LIZZIE

Queen of the Cattle Trails

LIZZIE

Queen of the Cattle Trails

by
Ann Fears Crawford

Illustrated by
Cheryl G. Fain

W.S. Benson & Company • Austin, Texas

FIRST EDITION

Text copyright © 1990 by Ann Fears Crawford
Illustrations copyright © 1990 by Cheryl G. Fain

Published in the United States of America
by W.S. Benson & Co., P.O. Box 1866, Austin, Texas 78767

ISBN 0-87443-091-7
Library of Congress Cataloging-in-Publication Data
Crawford, Ann Fears.
    Lizzie—Queen of the Cattle Trails/by Ann Fears
Crawford: Illustrated by Cheryl G. Fain.
    p. 60 cm. 24
    Bibliography: p. 60
    Summary: A biography of Lizzie Johnson Williams, pioneer
Texas cattle woman, who went up the cattle trail and made a
fortune.
    ISBN 0-87443-091-7: $12.95
    1. Williams, Lizzie Johnson, 1843(?)-1924—Juvenile litera-
ture. 2. Women ranchers—Texas—Juvenile literature. 3. Cattle
trails—Texas—Juvenile literature.
    (Williams, Lizzie Johnson, 1843(?)-1924. 2. Women ranchers—
Texas. 3. Cattle trails—Texas.)
I. Fain, Cheryl G., Ill. II. Title.
F391.W5C73.   1990
976.4'04'
(B)   89-82687
                        CIP   AC

for

WILLIAM

A very young Texan in the Far West

A Texas Girlhood

Many women dreamed of great adventures in frontier Texas. Most women who lived on the frontier homesteaded with their husbands, helped build homes, and reared their children.

Some women wrote books or stories for newspapers. Others wrote poems or composed music. Few women worked on ranches or worked cattle.

But Lizzie Johnson lived a life of high adventure in frontier Texas. She earned the title "Queen of the Cattle Trails" in the days when the cattleman was "king" in Texas.

Lizzie came to Texas as a young girl. Her father was a school teacher who brought his family to Texas from Missouri. In 1852 he built a log-cabin school house in Hays County, Texas.

While Lizzie's mother served meals to the students, Lizzie and her brother helped their father with the teaching duties.

Lizzie knew she would probably be a school teacher all her life, but she dreamed of a life of great adventure.

When the Civil War began, Lizzie's brother joined the Confederate Army. He marched off with other soldiers to fight for the South.

Lizzie was left at home to teach the students and to help her mother and sisters spin thread and make clothes for the soldiers.

Then the war ended, and Lizzie's father died. Her brother closed the Johnson Institute, and Lizzie moved to Austin to teach.

She carried her old roll book with her. Lizzie carefully wrote down student absences and notes on conduct in the book. She also wrote down her dreams and thoughts, putting her notes into the roll book.

DREAMS OF ADVENTURE

One day Lizzie had an idea. She would write her dreams of romance and adventure into stories.

Lizzie's stories were great successes. Soon she was selling her stories to a magazine in New York. Each month she would put away the money she made. She was saving money for her own adventures.

Then Lizzie took another job keeping books for a group of Texas cattlemen. She taught school during the day and worked on the books at night.

Still she found time to write her stories of romance and adventure.

Lizzie learned the ways of the cattle business. She learned that cattlemen often sold their herds by book count, not by the actual number in the herds.

This way the cattlemen often made huge profits on their cattle deals.

Lizzie enjoyed working for the cattlemen. She listened to their stories of life on the cattle trails and laughed at their jokes.

Lizzie picked up their old time sayings, and soon she was talking like a true Texas cowhand.

A Texas Cattlewoman

While Lizzie saved her money, she looked for a good investment. She wanted to make money, and she wanted to be part of the Texas cattle business.

Then Lizzie found a good investment. She bought part of a Chicago cattle business. She invested $2,000, and in three years she made $20,000.

Now Lizzie had enough money to buy cattle. She bought her own herd and the CY brand to go with it. Lizzie Johnson was in the cattle business!

Then Lizzie met the Reverend Hezekiah Williams and fell in love. "Hez's" wife had died, and he had grown sons.

Lizzie's brother often laughed at "Hez." He said that while "Hez" preached, his sons were out stealing the churchgoers' cattle.

But Lizzie loved Hez and they were married. Now her dreams of romance had come true.

But then Hez decided he wanted to be in the cattle business too. Unfortunately, Hez was not as good at business as Lizzie was. She always sold her cattle for more money.

Often Hez lost money on his herd. When he owed money to the bank, Lizzie paid his debt. But she always made Hez pay her back.

Lizzie and Hez lived on a ranch at Driftwood. But Lizzie kept a house in Austin. Here she ran her cattle business and kept track of her investments.

Lizzie won the respect of the Texas cattlemen. They knew she was a shrewd cattle dealer. Lizzie knew when to buy and when to sell. And she always bought good stock.

But even oldtime cattlemen were surprised when Lizzie decided to go up the trail with her cattle.

Up The Trail!

Few women in the West ventured up the cattle trail. Margaret Borland of Victoria went up the trail. She inherited her cattle herd from her husband.

Amanda Burks of Banquette also went up the trail, and Mary Taylor Bunton was a fine sight on the trail. She wove flowers in her hair and on her buggy. Then she went up the trail with her husband.

But cowhands talked about the hard life on the trail. They endured Texas northers with freezing wind and rain.

Often the sun shone hot and fierce. Cowhands wrapped bandanas around their mouths and noses to keep the dust out. They pulled their ten-gallon hats low over their eyes.

A cattle drive was often long and hard. It took many months to move a herd of cattle from ranch to market. Often the herd stretched out for more than two miles.

Cattle moved slowly. Cowhands rode beside the herd to move them ahead. They also rode in front and behind. Their horses were trained to keep the cattle in line.

Lizzie's cowhands were surprised that she wanted to go up the trail. Owning a cattle herd was one thing. Working cattle was quite another. Life on the trail was "no place for a lady," they said.

How would Lizzie act when the going got tough? What would happen when the herd had to cross a stream or river bed? Spring rains often flooded streams and rivers.

Would Lizzie's buggy get stuck in the mud? Would they have to pull it out? Would Lizzie be able to endure hard days and lonely nights on the trail? Would she cry herself to sleep?

But Lizzie surprised all the cowhands. Not only did she endure life on the trail, she seemed to revel in it.

She helped round up the herd. Then she recorded all the cattle in her tally book, making notes about the longhorns.

Then the day came for the herd to leave the ranch. Lizzie packed her buggy carefully. Into the buggy went her bedroll and one for Hez.

She packed picnic baskets with supplies. She even packed an umbrella. Lizzie was ready for storms on the trail.

Dressing for life on the cattle trail was a challenge even for Lizzie. She had to be prepared for dust storms, rain showers, and sudden northers.

Texas weather could change in an instant.

Hez watched Lizzie dress for the trail. He was amazed at the clothes she put on.

First, she put on a warm, red flannel petticoat. Then she added two muslin petticoats and a bright calico skirt.

Now Hez knew why cowhands called women "calicos."

Then Lizzie added a warm jacket over her blouse and wrapped herself in a warm shawl. Last of all, she popped on a bonnet to keep the sun out of her eyes.

Hez laughed and laughed. Lizzie looked like a stuffed pigeon! But Lizzie was ready at last to go up the cattle trail.

Finally the herd was ready. The riders saddled up. Lizzie and Hez climbed into their buggy.

"Let's ride out!" the trail boss called.

"Hit the trail! Let's ride! " the cowhands yelled.

"Ready, Lizzie?" asked Hez.

"Ready!" Lizzie replied.

Slowly the longhorns lumbered out. The cowhands urged the cattle on. The cow horses were raring to go.

The horses' hooves kicked up dust. Soon Lizzie and Hez were choking. Better to pull back or to ride up front, they decided.

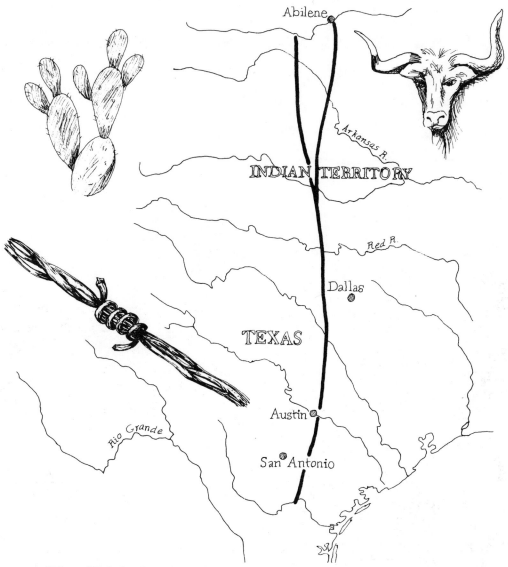

The Chisholm Trail was "a long haul," as the cowboys said. "Up the trail" was a good way to describe the famous cattle trail. It ran from Texas north to Kansas. It ran straight through Indian Territory.

Soon Lizzie forgot about the bouncing and jostling of the old buggy. She even forgot the choking dust that lodged in her throat and stung her eyes.

There was much to see on the cattle trail.

As the herd moved up the trail, scenery began to change. Soon the rocky, hill country lay far behind, and the herd headed for the open plains.

Lizzie and Hez saw many strange sights. The tall cactus plants stretched to the sky. Sagebrush bounced along the sandy grounds. Even the jackrabbits scurried out of sight as the herd went by.

When night fell, the moon rose, huge and white, in the sky. Stars sprinkled the cloudless sky.

Lizzie and Hez spread their bedrolls close to the campfire. Lizzie took off a few of her garments. She lay her bonnet, shawl, and jacket close by her bedroll.

But there was one more task still to be done.

One of the cowhands took his lariat from his saddle. Carefully he laid it around Lizzie and Hez's bedrolls. It made a huge circle on the ground.

"Snakes won't slither across an old rope," he told Lizzie. "They think that rope's just another old snake," he laughed.

Lizzie snuggled deep into her bedroll. The night grew cold. The horses were hobbled nearby. They whinnied at the night sounds.

Close by the campfire a few cowhands sat drinking the last of the coffee. Lizzie liked to listen to them tell tales of other journeys up the cattle trail.

One lone cowhand strummed a guitar. He sang a sad song of a cowboy's lost love and of lonely nights on the cattle trail.

The cowhands told stories of stampedes and dust storms, of broncos and brandings.

Always they talked of life on the trail and the cattle who kept them company.

Then the cowhands' voices grew quieter. Soon the campfire was only glowing embers, and all was quiet. Lizzie drifted off to sleep, happy and content on the Texas plains.

Before the sun was up, Lizzie was awake and dressed. She rolled her bedroll and placed it in the buggy.

With her tally book in hand, she carefully counted the cattle. None had strayed during the night. She also recorded each cowhand's hours in her time book.

When the trail boss rang the breakfast bell, Lizzie and Hez joined the cowhands around the chuckwagon.

The camp cook handed Lizzie an old tin plate. Then he heaped it with biscuits and bacon and gave her coffee in a tin cup.

Lizzie thought that the trail fare, eaten in the great outdoors, was the best food she had ever tasted.

It took many weeks of hard riding to get the herd to Kansas.

But Lizzie never forgot her duty. Each day she was up with the sun, making notes in her record books.

And she laughed and joked with the cowhands. She was delighted with the gifts they brought her. She enjoyed eating the wild fruit, prairie chicken, and antelope tongues.

When the tired, dusty cowhands led the longhorns into Wichita, Kansas, Lizzie found the trip well worth all the hard work.

She sold her cattle for a huge profit. Then she watched her longhorns loaded onto cattle cars. Soon they were off to markets in Chicago.

Then Lizzie and Hez traveled to St. Louis.

It was the first of many trips for the Texas ranch couple.

They stayed in fine hotels and ate fancy dinners. Then Lizzie went shopping.

For years she had studied drawings in magazines of elaborate dresses and hats. Now she could buy all she wanted.

Then Lizzie and Hez returned to Texas. Lizzie took great delight in paying back the money she owed the bank.

She wrapped her greenbacks in a red, bandana handkerchief. Then she walked down Congress Avenue to the bank.

One day Lizzie met Major George Littlefield, the founder of the bank. He was driving down the avenue in his buggy and doffed his hat to Lizzie.

Major Littlefield had made a great fortune in the cattle business. Lizzie smiled at the courtly gentleman and then shouted, "Hello, you old cattle thief!"

A Rich Woman

Lizzie sold more and more cattle. She went up the cattle trail often. She became rich, and she made many good investments.

She invested in city lots and in ranchlands. When the days of the Texas cattle trail ended, Lizzie was a very rich woman indeed!

Lizzie and Hez enjoyed traveling in style. They went many times to St. Louis and even to New York.

Lizzie bought fancy dresses and jewels. She liked to wear fancy hats trimmed with flowers, ribbons, and plumes.

Lizzie's favorite dress was very beautiful. It was a black silk dress with a bustle. It was trimmed with yards of black lace and glistened with jet beads.

Lizzie wore her dress to dinner parties and to the opera. But she was also a practical, Texas ranch woman. Among her purchases was a plain, gold watch. She wore it in a pocket at her waist. Lizzie wanted to be sure she never wasted time.

Then Lizzie and Hez took an exciting trip. They went to Cuba on business and stayed for a number of years.

When they returned to Texas, Lizzie brought back a surprise. She had a new pet—a talking parrot!

Then Hez became ill. Lizzie took him to Hot Springs and El Paso. She hoped the warm climate would cure him. But Hez died in El Paso.

Lizzie brought his body back to Austin. She bought him a fine casket and paid for his funeral.

Alone!

Now Lizzie was alone. She continued to invest her money wisely and to tend to business.

But she packed her fine dresses away and hid her jewels. She refused to go to parties or dances.

Although she had a good deal of money, Lizzie moved into a small apartment.

She bought a large amount of firewood, but would only burn one stick at a time.

At noon each day, Lizzie walked down the avenue. She
ate her lunch at the same cafe every day. She ate only one
dish—a bowl of vegetable soup.

When she finished her soup, she placed one dime beside
her plate and left.

When winter came, vegetables were hard to get. The owner of the cafe told Lizzie her soup would now be fifteen cents.

Lizzie refused. She made a deal with the owner. She told him she would eat her soup at his cafe every day for the next five years. But only if he would sell it to her for a dime.

The owner agreed. Lizzie had made another successful deal.

But Lizzie was growing old. She was ill and often imagined that she was back at the ranch. Or on the cattle trail.

She often dreamed that she was out on the plains under the open, Texas skies.

When Lizzie died, her relatives were amazed. They knew she owned land and buildings.

But they found that Lizzie had hidden money everywhere. They found thousands of dollars hidden in her bookcases. Her jewels were wrapped in a towel and stored in an unlocked box.

For years Lizzie's relatives told stories of their famous relative and the money she had made.

But the best stories were told by oldtime cowhands. They told stories of Lizzie's adventures on the Texas cattle trails. They remembered the old days when a "calico on the trail was as scarce as sunflowers on a Christmas tree."

But most of all, they remembered Lizzie Johnson. They remembered the Texas ranch woman who found a life of adventure and earned the title, "queen of the cattle trails."

WORDS TO KNOW

frontier	bandana	lariat
homestead	herd	snuggle
compose	endure	hobble
romance	round up	whinny
cattleman	tally book	strum
book count	longhorn	stampede
profit	petticoat	bronco
cowhands	calico	ember
invest	haul	stray
investment	territory	chuck wagon
debt	jostle	entry
respect	scenery	antelope
shrewd	plains	greenback
stock	cactus	doff
norther	sagebrush	courtly
fierce	scurry	opera

BOOKS ABOUT FRONTIER WOMEN
AND THE CATTLE TRAIL

Author, *Title*, Publisher

Crawford, *New Life, New Land: Women in Early Texas*, Eakin
Crawford and Ragsdale, *Women in Texas*, Eakin
Dobie, *Cow People*, Little, Brown & Company
Dobie, *The Longhorns*, Little Brown & Company
Exley, *Texas Tears and Texas Sunshine*, Texas A&M Press
Gard, *The Chisholm Trail*, University of Texas Press
Holland, *Brush Country Woman*, Texas A&M Press
Roach, *The Cowgirls*, Cordovan